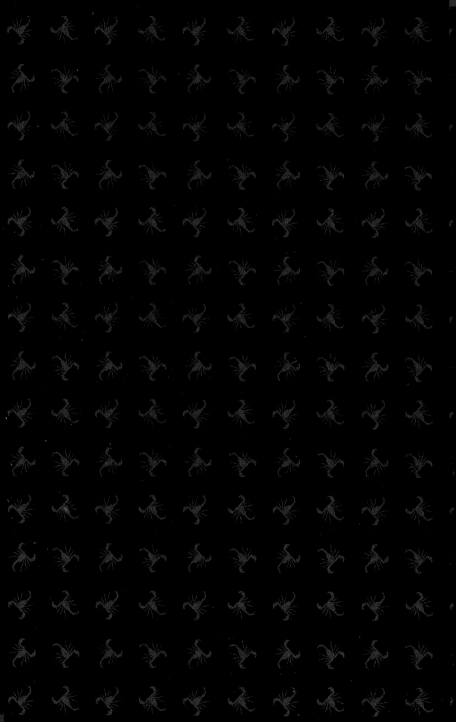

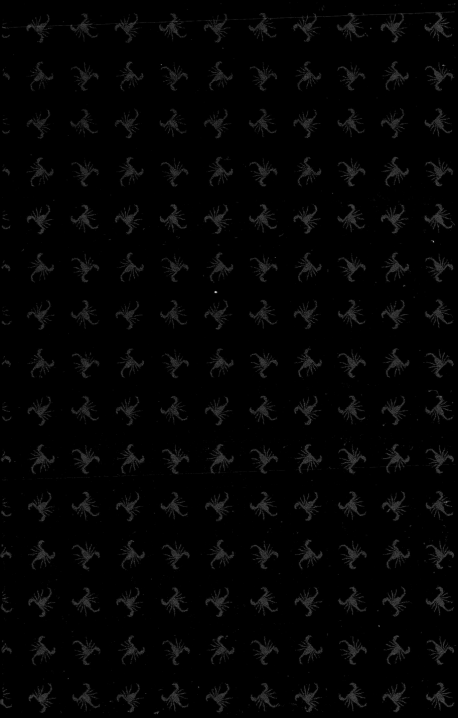

STEVE BORDEN

A.K.A. STING WITH GEORGE KING

NG

MOMENT OF TRUTH

COUNTRYMAN®

NASHVILLE, TENNESSEE

CONTENTS

PREFACE:

MOMENT OF TRUTH

For every person there is a Moment of Truth. In my job as a professional wrestler it always came in front of thousands of people in a crowded municipal auditorium or stadium or on television with twenty million people watching, waiting to see if I would survive the onslaught of my opponent. For the most part they came to see the underdog prevail against impossible odds. They were there for the story, because in many ways the story I projected in the ring reflected what they wanted to feel when the odds were against them in their own lives.

Everyone has had those moments when all the cards seem stacked against them, where there seems to be no hope. We want some miraculous surge of energy and resolve that allows us to triumph against all odds and save the day. That kind of imagery is what made wrestling one of the most watched sports in the world. What started out as a carnival sideshow turned into an athletic event that depends more on the story for its success than the official outcome of the contest.

What I discovered through my personal journey is that the ultimate Moment of Truth comes from the inside of a man as he begins to understand that he is not alone in the universe, that life just doesn't work unless it is connected to the living God. I found my Moment of Truth, or maybe I should say He found me. My life has never been the same. These pages tell you about a guy who gained everything the world calls success—and in

doing so almost lost his family, his life, and his immortal soul. This is a storyline that I could never have imagined. But praise God, the end of the story reads like the story in Luke 15 as a father receives a rebellious son with the open arms of grace. "For this my son was dead and is alive again; he was lost and is found" (Luke 15:24).

MAKING A MOVIE

Lots of people try to imagine what it would be like to be a star, to be famous. Many popular writers and speakers encourage their audiences to imagine that a movie is being made of their lives and that the movie will be shown on Judgment Day. The good, the bad, and the ugly of your life would be out there for everyone else to see. How would you change the script? Would you really want other people to see you so up-close and personal?

The truth is . . . making a movie about your life is just plain scary.

It took me a long time to get used to the idea that we actually were going to make a movie about my life. I thought, "Who cares? Can this really make a difference in people's lives?" One of the most difficult aspects of the process was to relive many of the things that had been so hurtful to both me and my family, but in the end my wife, Sue, and I became convinced that making this movie was exactly what God wanted us to do. As a new believer I want to make a difference in the world, and of late I have been spending much of my time in personal ministry alongside my brother Jeff, who has left his secure place in the corporate world to start a new church. I am an elder and get a lot of satisfaction out of serving. My dream is to take whatever notoriety I gained as a wrestler and give the glory back to God. I feel a real passion to bring the Gospel to unbelievers. Sue and I as a couple want to encourage other married couples to walk with Christ as they raise their families.

The movie is as much our story, as it is my story.

It is really amazing how God prepares our futures in ways we could not comprehend. A case in point is my friend Simeon Nix, who you will meet later in the book. It was Simeon who suggested I meet with Kathy King who he thought could help me in coordinating my desire to serve the Lord in the broader Christian community. Through Kathy I met her husband, George, and his partners Rob Venneri and Rick Wackeen at Dove Canyon Films. And the rest is history. The idea for a movie about my life started to be kicked around, and eventually I became comfortable with the idea of George, with whom I put this book together, writing and directing as my partner in the movie.

It took six months to write the screenplay. During that time George and I had lots of conversations and built a lot of trust that allowed Sue and me to open up our lives and tell our story in a God-honoring way. The one thing you need to know about the movie is that it is as much *our* story as it is my story. Through the process Sue and I learned a lot about each other, and we rejoiced in the salvation that had come to our family and the true healing that had come to our marriage through the mighty hand of God.

The casting process was interesting, because we decided that I was going to play myself as the most famous Sting persona, "the Crow." This meant that we had to recruit a young actor to play me in my early career when my look was completely different. When George said he had found a long-haired guitar player in Nashville who might fill the bill, I really didn't know how this kid was going to be transformed into a wild man wrestler. Then they cut Donnie Fallgatter's hair into my signature bleach blonde flat top, put him in some of my old costumes, and added my face paint, and what materialized was a

trip to the past. They mailed some pictures to our house that Sue opened up and left sitting on our kitchen table. When I passed by, I thought, "Where did those old pictures of me come from?" The likeness was startling.

A young actress named Liz Byler was chosen to play Sue. God worked out a time when Liz and Sue could get together awhile to talk about those days. Sue told her about her true feelings during the early days of our marriage, and that really made Liz's performance special. When Liz and Donnie began to work in front of the camera for the wedding scene, it brought back a lot of memories because it looked just like ours. They both did a great job.

George's partner Rob Venneri, a producer on the film, was my keeper during the shoot. He and I didn't know each other very well at the beginning, but as time went on we bonded and our families now hang out together some. Rob has a great wife, Cheryl, and kids who love the Lord. He is a maniac in a Christian kind of way with whom I share a love both for the Lord and for Starbucks.

The production schedule was crazy. Lots of shooting took place in an old movie studio that actually had been turned into a wrestling school. It was run by a guy named Bert Prentice who is a lifer in the wrestling business. Bert plays a wrestling school coach in the movie, and he has great presence on the screen. You could not have asked for a more perfect place to tell the story of the early days of my career. They made this place look like the little television studios where I wrestled when I was just getting started. Those were the days before Sting when I was known as "Flash Borden." I left Flash behind as soon as a better idea came along

Getting in the movie car really took me back to the day. The interior was exactly the same as the 1983 T-Bird I drove from California to Tennessee to begin my wrestling career. I think when I finally retired that car, it had over 177,000 miles on it.

We worked day and night, and I choreographed the wrestling segments. That was a lot of fun, especially because it was the other guys taking the "bumps" for a change. To see Donnie playing me in the ring and Ryan Wilson playing Jim Hellwig (my first tag-team partner) in our original makeup was like being in some kind of time warp. I got to show them a few of our original moves, which focused more on brute strength than finesse.

Then it was my turn to take the bumps, and I was in the ring as Sting "the Crow." I worked out with Chris Justice, a phenomenal wrestler. I've thought about doing a storyline with Chris if I ever go to WWE. He is at least 6'6 around 300 pounds. We worked out our studio match, and one move almost ended the movie. We decided to do one of Chris's signature moves that I had never done before. As cameras rolled I came off the ropes and we did the move. Being a little rusty made the timing of everything just a little off, and as a result the back of my head slammed to the canvas. I was knocked out cold. That had only happened to me one time before, and it is not a good feeling. Fortunately this time I was only out for a few seconds. Chris felt bad about the miss, but in truth it was my fault. When the disclaimer comes up before wrestling on TV—"don't try this at home"—it's the truth. After my head cleared, we picked up where we left off and finished the scene.

We shot day and night with the big dream sequence coming on the Wednesday of the first week a little before midnight. George had found an alley in an old oven factory that has been converted to a trendy shopping and dining spot in Franklin, Tennessee. It was the perfect location to realize this climactic scene, and the owner, Calvin Lehew, was very gracious to let us shoot there. I really liked the scene because it left lots of room for improvisation. I got to go a little crazy as I was being pursued in the dream by all the temptations that came at me when I was on the road. It was the middle of the night, and it was wild.

In the dream sequence I'm in a dark and smoky alley, the music is pounding, and everything is out of place. Even though I am supposed to be asleep in my hotel room, I find myself locked out of the coliseum where I had just wrestled. I notice a reflection in a dirty pane of glass and see that I am still in my full Sting garb. I begin to run, and the camera moves with me as the grips clear the cables so no one will fall and hurt themselves. Women of the evening beckon me, but I run screaming away from them.

At this point while we were filming, George yelled for me to climb a vine-covered trellis up to the factory roof. It was like a stunt in the ring—once you make the commitment in your mind, your reflexes take over and you just go for it. I climbed as fast as I could, appearing as frantic as possible. Once I got up there I worked the edge of the roof, pretending to almost fall off the building. The crew and extras on the ground watching really freaked out because only George and the director of photography, Lew Chanatry, and I knew what was happening. We made up this part of the scene as we went, and it made everyone really nervous, especially the insurance people. But what seemed so dangerous to them was really all in a day's work in my normal wrestling world. As the scene continued, I climbed off the roof and continued my frantic run, pausing once to peer through a window that had light streaming out into the night, then falling backwards over a pile of metal. Everyone in the alley starts chasing me at this point, and the music starts blasting. Really exciting stuff.

In the next-to-last scene in the movie, I finally surrender to the Lord Jesus, and we only shot that scene once. I let go of everything and pleaded with God for salvation. Reliving the moment of surrender to the mighty hand of God was like feeling His chisel all over again. All the feelings of desperation came back. I felt the pain and fear of being without hope and the realization that without God I was doomed. That scene was a true expression of my desperate heart receiving the love and forgiveness that only comes through a repentance of sin and the need for a Savior. Usually I waited to hear the director say "let's do one more," but after we finished the first take there was just silence; he knew I laid it all on the line and there was nothing left to give. Everyone just left the room quietly, because we all knew the Spirit of God had truly anointed that moment. There was no second take.

> It was like a stunt in the ring—once you make the commitment in your mind, your reflexes take over and you just go for it.

GROWING UP

There was nothing like growing up in Southern California, where fun is an art form.

My family came out from Nebraska. My grandpa was a hard-working guy who loved body building. We didn't get to see him very much, but when he did visit us we would always get out the old books and pictures of him and his buddies, one of whom was Steve Reeves who played Hercules in the movies. My parents worked really hard keeping a roof over our heads and food on the table. The whole family was into sports, and Mom and Dad never missed a game. When I was 8 or 9 my mom got involved in a Bible study and made a profession of faith in Christ. She started to take us to church, but with no support from the rest of the family, our churchgoing was sporadic at best.

I was the oldest child. Then came my brother Jeff, our sister Kelley, and lastly our brother Mark. There could not have been two guys more different than Jeff and me. He pushed all the limits, while I did everything I could to not make waves. We both were running from God in our own ways. Jeff was on a path that could have ended his life early age, which would have crushed our parents, but in reflecting on what eventually happened, I was the one who actually was more in danger of losing my life.

> *My interest as a kid was sports, and as I grew into my teenage years I added girls and friends to my "what's important" list.*

My interest as a kid was sports, and as I grew into my teenage years I added girls and friends to my "what's important" list. By the time I got to high school, I really focused on basketball. I dreamed of going to college for basketball, but I didn't pay enough attention to my grades for that to become a reality. So I ended up at College of the Canyons for two years. It was a little humiliating but a good lesson about the results of not paying the price for what you want. After those two years I was worn out on school and decided I didn't need college to go where I wanted to go.

After trying college for a while, I worked as a bouncer, swimming pool builder, bartender, and health club owner.

Not going to college did not mean that I was short on dreams. As a kid I'd dreamed of playing professional basketball, football, or baseball, but in my early twenties I followed my grandfather's passion by packing on the muscle in the gym. I reasoned that if I could get my body into good enough shape, maybe I could break into the movies. Arnold Schwarzenegger was the greatest bodybuilder any of us had ever seen, and building a physique like that became my goal for making my way into Hollywood.

All of life is about building relationships, and none of us really knows the path where God is leading us. After trying a few other things, I became an expert in the gym business, and a buddy of mine named Ed Connors invited me to be his partner in Gold's Gym. That is really the beginning of the story. I worked on bodybuilding every day. We drew lots of people to the gym, and we were having some success. But the dreams I'd had as a kid stuck with me, and I thought bodybuilding might be my ticket to one day entertaining thousands of people.

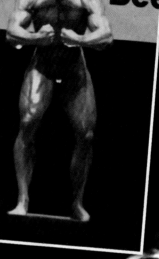

THE HULK & BLUE SPANDEX

Then something happened that on the surface was just a small diversion in a day's work, but looking back I realize now that God was setting the course of my life even though I did not yet know Him personally. On this day of destiny, a guy named Terry and his wife came into the gym to work out. My staff went crazy, and I thought that Terry must be someone famous. The man they were talking about had a really good body, a charismatic smile, and a genuinely nice personality. As it turned out he was the "Hulk"—Hulk Hogan, the reigning king of professional wrestling. Little did I know that our paths would cross again and that it would lead to the biggest pay per view event of all time.

As the HulkaMania settled down at the gym, I forgot about wrestling until another knock came to my door in the person of Rick Bassmen. Rick came into the gym with three really big athletes, and he told me he was going to shape those guys into a wrestling phenomenon. I was a little skeptical about the phenomenon part, but I was very happy to sell them some gym time. Rick would come in with his guys, and he began to tell me just how much money there was to be made for the right wrestlers who understood what people were looking for in the ring. Well, Rick could sell ice to Eskimos, and after a few visits to the gym he pitched me about joining his wrestling troupe. I liked the money part of the conversation, and I was looking for a change that would take my life someplace new. When Rick told me that he'd found an investor who would pay my way to wrestling camp, I finally said "yes."

I began to learn about a whole new world that I had never imagined. A lot of my Southern California friends must have thought I'd lost my mind. To me, this looked like a way to become financially independent. I had a lot to learn.

On the way to wrestling school, one of Rick's big guys dropped out. Rick was really insistent that we should have four big guys on the squad, so I suggested we call this monster of a man I had met named Jim Hellwig. He was a bodybuilder who had won the Mr. Georgia contest. Jim showed up driving a beautiful Mercedes and looking like he had just won the lottery; he had left his profession as a chiropractor to give wrestling a shot.

Rick took us to the wrestling Yoda of California, Red Bastien, who was an agent for Vince McMahon, Sr., in the ring. Red was a tough guy with a handlebar mustache. He was around 70 years old and he took his job very seriously. I remember the first day we started taking bumps. A "bump" in the wrestling business is a very gentle-sounding term for what happens when your body slams into the canvas or table or floor or anything else that happens to be in the way. We would learn basic moves and then practice them over and over again.

Red occasionally would let us throw him around the ring as he taught us. One of the basic power moves he taught us is called the "vertical suplex." It is very simple but looks really spectacular to the audience. Basically you pick your opponent up over your head and then fall backward, smashing him to the mat on his back. Well, old Red let us suplex him as we were learning. Why, I will never know. After one session I asked him if he had ever been hurt while wrestling. He just stopped right there, dropped his sweat pants a little, and showed us two big scars from where he'd had both hips replaced. It was a little strange to know we had been smashing around a 70-year-old man who'd been through that. A lot of people believe there is some kind of special padding up there in the ring floor that makes it not hurt when you hit the deck. I discovered this was a myth—when your all-muscle frame hits the deck, it hurts each and every time. Red kept reinforcing the fact that if we would learn everything we needed to learn from him, we probably wouldn't get killed.

Midway through the wrestling camp, Rick decided it was time for us to see big-time wrestling, so he took us on a little field trip into Los Angeles. There we piled out of the car wearing bright blue spandex tights, Gold's Gym T-shirts, and matching white wrestling shoes. Our dress was a little strange even by L.A. standards as we marched right up to the ticket window and into a world I had never seen except on my aunt's television in Nebraska when I was 9. The whole place was ablaze in the red and yellow of HulkaMania. The all-star card also included Andre the Giant, the British

Bulldogs, Big John Stud, the Iron Sheik, and many others. Rick's instincts were right on target—we were mobbed by fans who assumed we were already famous. It was a good lesson for me about perception and reality. We signed hundreds of autographs, and I could see this business had a lot of potential. I thought it was the wrestlers who were making the money. That was only slightly true.

Rick could sell ice to Eskimos, and after a few visits to the gym he pitched me about joining his wrestling troupe.

That was an eye opener, and we four big rookies knew just enough to be dangerous. Seeing the fans go crazy for Hulk started a whole process of understanding in me about what wrestling was all about. It dawned on me that wrestling was about the fans, about forming a relationship with them in such a way that they would be attracted to your character. That they would admire not just what you did in the ring, but what you stood for in there. This ongoing revelation served me well throughout my career.

We immediately got some promotional pictures made of the four-man wrestling attraction known as the "Freedom Fighters," and we sent

We were mobbed by fans who assumed we were already famous. It was a good lesson for me about perception and reality.

the pictures out to promoters all over the country. Only one response came back. Jerry Jarrett, who ran the territory known as the Championship Wrestling Association (CWA), was interested. Those were the days before big television and pay per view, and the country was basically divided up among entrepreneurs who complied with a gentlemen's agreement not to compete with each other in certain parts of the country. The South and the Midwest at that time were the center of the wrestling world, and we were fortunate to be part of the Nashville-based CWA.

Although we had trained as the four Freedom Fighters, Mr. Jarrett only wanted the two big guys on the left of the picture—Jim Hellwig and me. That was the way of the wrestling world. The promoter was the top rung of the business, and he was always looking for the next big thing that would draw people to his wrestling shows. He had all the leverage. This was show business.

The more that Jim and I talked with Mr. Jarrett, the more we began to feel that the big bucks were just around the corner. Then he asked something that should have sent me running back to the health club: "Do you have a car?" Not only were we going to drive from California to Nashville, but that great symbol of personal independence, the automobile, would be our major mode of transportation—and sometimes my personal address—as we traveled from city to city plying our new trade. Until that moment I had considered myself an intelligent man, but I guess Mr. Jarrett's Southern accent hypnotized me. I was a guy who was born in Nebraska and raised in Southern California; I had never seen grits and thought deep frying only happened to french fries. My worldview was about to change. When I told everyone I was headed for Nashville, they must've all thought I was out of my mind.

JEFF

I need to tell you about my brother Jeff so that you can understand my journey. God has used him in a big way in my life. When I think about how different we were growing up, it is a wonder we have any communication, much less a life as bonded brothers in Christ. We attended Peachland Elementary, Placerita Junior High, and Hart High School, and we both aggressively played organized football, baseball, and basketball. Jeff made a statement to the world by how he wore his hair, the music he listened to, the friends he chose, and the habits he developed. I carefully managed my reputation and was very peer-conscious; Jeff on the other hand didn't give a rip about what anybody thought. One thing we both shared was that we were very high on our own opinions. I was a full blown jock, and Jeff was rowdy and free spirited. Our relationship was really strained because of the affect his life was having on our mom and dad. They really worried about him! However, I was a wolf in sheep's clothing, doing my own thing and loving it. The Borden Brothers were fearless on every front.

With my brother's background, you can imagine my surprise and genuine wonderment that he had gone to an Easter musical at a church with our parents and his new girlfriend (who later became his wife, Lori) and accepted Christ as his personal Savior!

Before then, only our mom knew the Lord, and our parents had been nominal churchgoers. When Jeff made his announcement everyone who knew him was floored, especially the friends with whom he had partied for so long. That night our dad professed Christ for the first time as well. Jeff's whole life radically changed overnight, and I believed I had lost the brother I had known my whole life. I thought he had gone off his rocker. This was about eighteen months before I left for Nashville. Jeff wanted the Lord more than anything, and he talked openly about his newfound faith. He started to be a Bible-memorization machine. God completely healed him of his addictions and gave him a mind for the Word of God. I witnessed this miracle with my own eyes.

Then about two weeks before my big trip east, Jeff led our sister Kelley to the Lord, and

suddenly I was on the outside looking in at the family
I thought I knew. They were
all different because of their
faith in the Savior. That

was nice for them, I thought, but it all sounded a
little confining for a guy like me who was ready to
go out and beat the world. That left only one family
member I could relate to, my brother Mark, because
neither of us knew the Lord.

My radically saved brother tried to dissuade me
from going to Nashville, but once he
realized my mind was made up, he
wrote me a letter to let me know where
he stood and how much he loved me.
Although its content reinforced the
awkwardness in our relationship at the
time, I kept the letter, and it is still
a real treasure for me almost twenty
years later. In the letter Jeff said that
God had His eye on me and that no
matter how far I roamed, nothing
would be able to separate me from the love of God
which is in Christ Jesus our Lord (Romans 8:39).

*When Jeff
made his
announcement
everyone who
knew him was
floored.*

He said if I would repent of my sins and name Jesus as my Savior, I would be changed from the inside out. Jeff also promised he would always be there for me. That was the beginning of what became a fifteen-year process of God hunting me down to make me His son.

Some of you have family members for whom you have been praying for a very long time. Maybe you've begun to feel like it doesn't matter if you continue to pray or not. Jeff prayed for me every day for fifteen years, and I know he must have said to himself many times, "Will this knucklehead ever get it?" Let me tell you from the viewpoint of a man who was headed for hell and now isn't—don't give up. Keep on praying.

The Bible often uses the phrase "in due time" when referring to how God in His love waits patiently for us to understand His grace. I was prayed for without fail by a brother, sister, mother, and father, who all loved God and loved me, and "in due time" those prayers were answered not only for me,

Suddenly I was on the outside looking in at the family I thought I knew. They were all different because of their faith in the Savior.

but for my whole family. "Pray without ceasing" (1 Thessalonians 5:17).

Jeff, Dad, and Steve

Let me tell you from the viewpoint of a man who was headed for hell and now isn't— don't give up. Keep on praying.

For when we were still without strength, in due time Christ died for the ungodly.

ROMANS 5:6

SUE

I had one other qualm about leaving town—a girl had stolen my heart, and I had asked her to marry me. Her name was Sue.

Our story starts while I was tending bar at what was then a happening spot, Victoria's Station, a restaurant and night club just outside of the Universal Studios lot. I was a bouncer who graduated to bartender. Bartending really appealed to me, because it allowed me to be a little crazy and put on a show for the customers I served, which resulted in very good tips. Among the food servers in the restaurant was a girl who I was drawn to immediately; I couldn't take my eyes off her. The first time she came to the bar to get change from me, I not only had a crush on her, but I thought, "I could marry this girl." She was so shy and soft spoken yet confident.

I believe one of God's most enjoyable duties is to teach us that people who on the surface seem to be polar opposites are actually drawn to each other in some unexplainable way that brings balance, especially in our

There could not have been two more opposite people then Sue and me. . . . all I knew for sure is that I wanted to marry her.

marriages, and there could not have been two people more opposite then Sue and me. I was a night owl, loved to get together with my friends, and party until the wee hours of the morning. The bartending life seemed perfect for my well-developed party skills. I was living the life, and I was definitely a player.

Then New Year's Eve came and a co-worker named John Resh knew Sue and I were interested in each other, so he commenced to hook us up. There we were cashing out for the night and almost alone for the first time. John moved the situation along, as he told Sue about a customer who was hitting on her.

He said within my hearing, "She would never go out with that guy."

I asked, "What guy?"

And John replied, "Steve, why are you so interested? She would never go out with a guy like you either." As John walked away he knew he had set us up.

I asked Sue, "Is that true you wouldn't go out

with a guy like me?"

She answered, "Why don't you ask me?" so I did. And she said yes!

Love at first sight might or might not be real, whether it's right or wrong I can't say, but all I knew for sure was that I wanted to marry Susan W. Himes. She was a one-man kind of girl who had recently come out of a long-term relationship and was not in the market to get hurt again. She liked quiet, private little dinners and meaningful conversation, and I liked that too. The rub in our relationship came as I wanted to also go out with friends from the bar but didn't want Sue to be part of that scene. I didn't want the girl I introduced to my parents to be part of that party life.

Our relationship continued to grow against all odds, as I was committed not to change. Sue's father was very refined. He stood six-foot-four-inches and was very handsome. He came to Hollywood as an accomplished stage actor with a dream to be a leading man in the movies. Although his dream did not go as he had planned, he can be seen in a character part in *Executive Action* and other films. Sue's mother is a beautiful woman who was also an actress. She had a role in a 60s movie, *Love and Kisses*, with Ricky Nelson the singer, who had grown up on television with his famous parents Ozzie and Harriet and his brother David. Sue was definitely Daddy's little girl. I don't think he was especially pleased when she brought home this bodybuilding bartender who wanted to follow Arnold Schwarzenegger into Hollywood as the next muscleman turned action star. Some men become better people when they are trying to win a woman's heart, but my strategy was a little different. I decided to be myself no mater what. The miracle was that the chemistry between us was so strong that me being myself didn't stop us from falling head over heels in love.

I never had wanted to marry any girl except for Sue. She was the ONE.

Sue's parents were polite and learned to accept me, but after three years Sue grew weary of being what she felt was second place in my life to the friends and the gym I now co-owned. To my amazement she unceremoniously dumped me because I wouldn't change. Even though I knew Sue was the one, I still wasn't ready to give up my lifestyle.

We both started seeing other people, but we were miserable without each other. After a few months, I got up the guts to call Sue, and I promised her I would be different; I would change. She agreed to give me another chance. In the single most romantic thing I have ever done before or since, I put together enough money to buy a ring. I took her to lunch at the Hotel Hotel Bel-Air, got down on one knee, and asked Sue to be my wife. With a big beautiful smile on her face she told me how much she loved me and said, "Yes!"

Some men become better people when they are trying to win a woman's heart... but I decided to be myself no matter what.

Neither Sue or I could have ever anticipated how different things would become. One week later Rick Bassmen walked into the gym, and everything started to be crazy.

I can't imagine the response Sue got when she informed her parents that the man she was going to marry had just dyed his hair orange, shaved two lighting bolts in the side of his head, and was going to school to be a professional wrestler. She might as well have said I was leaving town to join the circus, which was closer to the truth than I could have imagined. If my beautiful daughter, Gracie, made such an announcement, my resulting reaction might not be something that would make Jesus smile. Thank God that as of this writing Gracie is only four years old, so such an encounter is years off, if ever.

> *Sue might as well have told her parents I was leaving town to join the circus, which was closer to the truth than I could have imagined.*

Sue and I were not Christians, but we were in love, and real love has a spiritual quality. We were crazy about each other, and Sue was willing to put up with this wild wrestling idea because she loved me.

As Jim and I left town, I promised Sue that I would bring her to Nashville as soon as I could get established. We burned up the phone line talking to each other. (This was before e-mail, when actually talking to each other was still in vogue.) The long distance romance only intensified our desire to be together, and I thought May 18, 1986, could not come soon enough.

Sue and I were not Christians,
but we were in love,
and real love has a spiritual quality.

THE ROAD

You never know how big this country is until you drive it non-stop. It would have been nice to be in Jim's big Mercedes, but Jim had gotten rid of it. So there we were loading up the '83 T-Bird. Jim and I had just enough money to get to Nashville if we didn't stop at any hotels, so we decided to drive it straight through. Our adrenaline had started to run out as we came across the New Mexico high country and ran smack into a blizzard. We hit a patch of ice and spun three 360s without hitting anyone or anything. We were so burned by then that neither of us said anything; we just looked straight ahead and kept on driving. We pressed across the panhandle of Texas, up through Arkansas, across the Mississippi River into Memphis, and then on to Nashville.

Jim is a unique guy with his own ideas about everything, which made for an interesting first trip together. Both of us were young, big, and ripped, so we got stared at whenever we got out of the car. We also were both hungry all the time. Jim talked all about the food in the

South, and he made the Waffle House sound like the eating equivalent of the Land of Oz. When we finally pulled up under the first black and yellow sign I was kind of underwhelmed, but Jim jumped from the car with the excitement of a kid at Christmas. I was not prepared for the eating frenzy we were about to undertake. Jim started with two pecan waffles, with four eggs and syrup on top. And then a ham and cheese omelet, hash browns smothered with cooked onions, and toast on the side. Of course there was milk and lots of coffee. This was his standard meal every time we stopped at Waffle House for the next two years. The Waffle House will smother anything on the menu with fried onions, cheese, or sausage gravy, and the frequent result is a gastronomic adventure that should never be spoken of in polite company.

When we finally arrived in Nashville we went directly to Jerry Jarrett's house. It was a beautiful home with a majestic staircase that curved to the second floor from the black and white marble tile in the foyer. He immediately took us to his home studio to record a television promo. Two other wrestlers, who were dripping with gold jewelry, were already in there cutting interviews. I learned right then and there that television was a huge part of the wrestling game. You would wrestle once a week on television and set up the storyline for the next week. Then you would go out on the road every night in a different city and play the storyline out in front of a live audience. Your television match created the advertising for your appearances. Our first promo was a little rough, but it did tell fans that the Freedom Fighters were now part of Jerry Jarrett's Mid-South wrestling show. You could hear the wheels turning in Mr. Jarrett's head as he made plans for getting the most out of the two freaks from the West Coast. The gimmick was us—we lit up the whole room when we strode in wearing our red, white, and blue faces and colorful spandex; I'm sure we gave veteran wrestlers a good laugh. Then Mr. Jarrett told us that the Freedom Fighters would be on television the

> Television was a huge part of the wrestling game. You would wrestle once a week on television and set up the storyline for the next week. Then you would go out on the road every night in a different city and play the storyline out in front of a live audience.

next morning at channel 5 in Memphis—another four-hour drive.

I honestly can't remember who Jim and I wrestled the first time there in Memphis, but I can tell you it was ugly. We picked them up over our heads and dropped them simultaneously to the mat. In 45 seconds flat, it was all over. Another great moment in television wrestling history. Then we drove on to Jonesboro, Arkansas, that evening for our first real match. That began a driving jamboree that seemed to never end. Jim and I became a popular sideshow, but in retrospect it is humorous to think how green and awful we really were.

I was desperate for Sue, and she finally came out for a visit. At the time I was sharing a house with Jim and his wife, Sheri, just off Music Row in Nashville. Sue was excited to be with me, and sharing an apartment with another couple didn't bother her. What did bother her was when Jim and I had to leave town for almost a month. Sheri began to tell Sue about what life was really like being married to a wrestler. This should

> *Jim and I became a popular sideshow, but in retrospect it is humorous to think how green and awful we really were.*

have given Sue some warning about our future. Sue has often said that whenever she wanted to throw in the towel on our relationship, she would hear Sheri's voice in her head telling her she would never make it, and that memory would bring out Sue's stubborn streak. Isn't it amazing how God took words that weren't meant for the good of our marriage and turned them around for something positive? Over the years, we've seen a lot of that.

The money had not started to roll in as we had hoped. I was making just $25 to $50 a night, and I had to deduct expenses like gas, food, and God forbid you stayed overnight somewhere. That meant there would be at least four huge wrestlers in one room of dubious quality. I always brought a blender along, though, to make a protein drink. The older wrestlers knew all the cheap, decent places, but many a night the car looked mighty good to me. During those four months the Freedom Fighters went through a name change as Mr. Jarrett tried to grow our popularity with his crowds. We became the

Blade Runners—out with the red, white, and blue war paint, and in with the black. But what Jim and I really needed was some seasoning that would give us finesse in the ring instead of just brute force. We were developing the reputation of being awkward and hurting other wrestlers. Then I separated my shoulder, which gave Mr. Jarrett the way out he was looking for, to "finish us up," as they say.

One of the secrets to keeping the wrestling crowds happy was introduce new talent to the fans. I learned early on that you had to keep reinventing yourself to keep your job. I think Mr. Jarrett liked us, but we would need a lot more experience. Mr. Jarrett did a gracious thing in calling up Cowboy Bill Watts, a legend in the wrestling world who at that time owned the United Wrestling Federation (UWF). Although

> I frankly have no idea why Sue stuck with me, but I thank God she did.

There's a scene in the movie where Young Sting opens a can of tuna, puts it into a blender, and then fills the blender with orange juice. This was my protein drink of choice—cheap, filling, and effective for growing muscles. As people have seen the film, this is a moment when every women curls up her nose and every guy says to himself "I could do this."

the UWF was based in Tulsa, Oklahoma, most of Bill's wrestlers lived in Alexandria, Louisiana, which was right in the middle of the states where Bill promoted.

By the time Jim and I moved, Sue had gone home to prepare for our wedding. I frankly have no idea why she stuck with me, but I thank God she did.

Jim and I were real health nuts. We guzzled an orange juice and tuna protein drink almost every day to keep up our physiques, but from time to time we would "party at the Waffle House." I began to look forward to the breakfast extravaganza that had very few things that a bodybuilder actually should eat.

I'll give you a little inside scoop on the movie. In the movie they mistakenly put the Blade Runners' war paint on the Freedom Fighters. The Freedom Fighters' gimmick was those red, white, and blue spandex tights in a world where most wrestlers wore black. When I realized it was the wrong paint job, those scenes had already been put to bed. Hard core wrestling historians— I think there are a few—will catch that flub, and it will be a hot topic on the Internet for about two minutes.

The Blade Runners' war paint gave us sort of an extraterrestrial look. It got us noticed. During that time, not only did I change my ring name to Sting, but Jim also changed his name from Jim Justice to Rock. Jim now is best-known as The Ultimate Warrior.

THE MARRIED MAN

I finally went home to Santa Clarita to get married.

About three weeks before going home, I had gotten a terrible staph infection. Although I was taking medication, I was still wrestling every day and using gyms and showers that were rather less then sterile. I called Sue ten days before the wedding to tell her how sick I was. In those three weeks I lost twenty-seven pounds. When I finally got home my family and friends were really worried, and I know they discussed how I had blown it by leaving town to go wrestle. There was no way anyone could grasp what I was really going through. My pride kept me from saying how really rough I was feeling until my brother Mark and sister Kelley found me groaning on the couch and took me to the emergency room to get help.

But on a beautiful May 18, surrounded by Jeff and his new wife, my folks, Sue's folks, and lots of our friends, Sue and I were married outside by a lake. Sue was radiant as she glided to me in her wedding dress—the most beau-

tiful woman I had ever seen. I could see the difference in my family, especially Jeff, but I was too worried about having a new bride and a new boss to notice much. When Sue and I first watched our wedding scene as played in the movie by actors Donnie Falgatter and Liz Byler, it was truly *deja vu*.

I had to go back to work almost immediately, and the plan was for Sue to follow me as soon as I had enough money for us to get an apartment of our own. We promised each other that we would take a real honeymoon after the big money started rolling in. (Our honeymoon in Puerto Vallarta, Mexico, was a bust because we both got food poisoning.) When you are an optimist, you are an optimist—it was two months before my bride finally came to be with me.

During our first six months with Cowboy Bill, Jim and I started to gain some popularity, and we began to do the main events. Bill Watts dreamed up a storyline with former pro football player Ernie Ladd that really worked, and we did nine nights of nearly sell-out crowds. Jim and I figured our take for those nights would be about $950 dollars each, but when we finally got the checks they were for half that much. When you subtracted our housing and travel, we made almost nothing. Jim and I were sitting backstage, all dressed and ready to go and do our match, when we found out about the money. We stormed out of the arena and left Bill high and dry.

The next day I got a call from Grizzly Smith, Bill's number one agent, asking me what happened, and I told him we just couldn't live on the money we were making. He said if that I would do the match the next night, all would be forgiven. He also said they did not want Jim back. What I didn't know was that Jim had brokered a deal with another promoter and was planning our exit anyway. Well, I decided to take the risk and go do the match. This was a big risk; I had heard of wrestlers who walked out in the past who got hurt really bad the next time they went into the ring. I was assured that no retribution would be taken against me, and they set me to wrestle a solo match with the man himself—Cowboy Bill Watts, my boss and the reigning champion of our wrestling federation. Bill had this one move where he draped your legs spread eagle in the corner over the ropes; then he would look like

> When you are an optimist, you are an optimist. It was two months before my bride finally came to be with me.

he was kicking parts of the anatomy a newlywed would especially want to keep. But Bill was true to his word and nobody got hurt.

I collected a couple of back paychecks and used that money to rent my own apartment—I was ready to bring my beautiful bride to scenic Alexandria, Louisiana. The trip home to get married had taken what little money I had in reserve, so the furniture I had planned to buy had not materialized. I know Sue would have really loved for me to carry her over the threshold into our candlelit home the way it is depicted so romantically in the movie, but I couldn't even afford candles. We had no candles and absolutely no furniture. None. No couch, no kitchen table, no chairs, just some blankets made to look like a bed on the floor. We had a fork I had taken from a hotel along the way and plain white towels that came from another hotel. We also had a clock radio. But being young and optimistic and hopeful for the future does carry you for a while.

Our first home was at the Pine Crest Apartments on the outskirts of Alexandria, where some of the other wrestlers and their families lived. It was next to a paper mill, which could explain why the rent was so "reasonable." If you have never experienced a paper mill's  aroma, I can assure you **that smell will** never be a cologne.

Two days after Sue got there, I had to take our only car on the road for thirty days straight, so Sue had no way to go out and look for a job. She was just stuck at the empty apartment. Her only contact was with the other wrestling wives. Fortunately for our marriage, Sue made friends with Lori, the wife of my new tag-team partner, Rick Steiner. This became the medicine Sue needed to not go stark raving mad. Lori has a great sense of humor, and she and Sue developed a contest to see who could smash the largest cockroach in the apartment. They even had a specially designated tennis shoe that they used to bring destruction to the bug population. I should mention, though, that we eventually did go to Mr. Steve's furniture rental, with the first thing we rented being, what else, a television. I think the bed came second.

One of the more memorable moments during our

stint in Louisiana was when I was booked to wrestle at a county fair. I was scheduled for the next to last match. The sun was going down and the lights they'd turned on were going dim, so the local promoter got on the microphone and said, "Now ladies and gentlemen, as you can see, it's getting a little hard to see the ring, because we don't seem to have enough juice to make the lights work right. So what I want you to do is pull some of your cars up and surround the ring. And if you wouldn't mind, would you please turn on your high beams?" The smell of livestock and exhaust left a permanent scar on my memory. This was not the glamorous life; it was just plain hard work.

Being young and optimistic and hopeful for the future does carry you for a while.

The "Cowboy" filmed his television events from Tulsa, Oklahoma, and when we went to Tulsa we always did a midday show in Oklahoma City also. At other times we would film some big shows in Houston. The Blade Runners had been retired when Jim left, and my Sting persona was really catching on. I teamed up with Rick Steiner and Eddie Gilbert in a storyline where we won the UWF tag-team cham-

"*God draws the mighty away with His power;*
He rises up, but no man is sure of life.
He gives them security, and they rely on it;
Yet His eyes are on their ways."

JOB 24:22-23

from the film STING: Moment of Truth

pionship. Then I broke with them and became a good guy. This really resonated with the fans.

About this time Cowboy Bill hung up his wrestling spurs and sold his operation to a competitor, Jim Crockett and his North American Wrestling Association. The NWA was the next big leap for my young career, and we were told that we were moving to Dallas. Sue and I first got another apartment there, and then we decided to jump in way over our heads and buy a little house. The NWA offered me something I had never had up to this point in my career—a real contract that guaranteed me pay every week. Even with a salary and the fame that started coming by being on the TBS network, owned by a young television maverick named Ted Turner, Sue and I couldn't afford the mortgage, so we decided to rent a room to a wrestler known as the Angel of Death. But the extra money and Sue's job still weren't enough to keep us afloat.

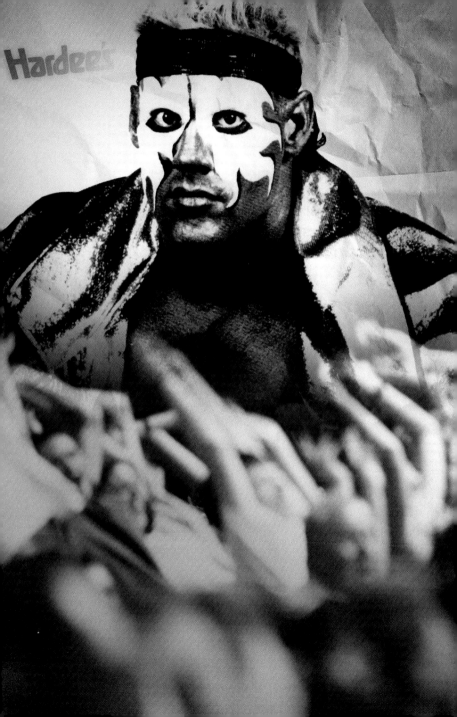

THE BREAK

Desperation is one of God's best tools to get your attention. All of us can remember times when we tried to be masters of our own worlds and we made a complete mess out of it. That's where I was. I felt like my career was on the verge of a breakthrough, and yet there we were in that little house with another person living there so we could make the mortgage. If working hard was the answer, then Sue and I should have been millionaires. I was commuting every week to Atlanta or to Charlotte, North Carolina, where the NWA shot its weekly TBS show, and then I would hit the road and leave Sue to fend for herself. We just couldn't work hard enough to get ahead. One night Sue and I were coming across I -10 on our way home from a match, and after staring through the night in silence for a while I said to her, "Why don't we just leave this behind and keep going? We can be home in three days." For a minute it was like I could actually smell the ocean. But Sue was my biggest fan and assured me that things would get better if we just stayed the course. So

I turned the car and headed back to our house in Arlington.

Things didn't get better. I was away more and more, and the expenses of travel ate up what I earned even though my fame was growing. A turning point came one night when Sue went to bed early and I had a rare night alone. There came a moment that was so out of character for me that I'll never forgot it. I was in the kitchen of that little house, all alone brooding over our financial condition and lack of momentum in my career that I thought my efforts deserved. What started out as a pity party turned into a pleading with God. I really hadn't given God much consideration in any decision I had ever made. But as I had watched my brother Jeff and the other members of my family, I'd begun to realize that maybe God could be a help after all. I thought maybe God and I could make a deal, so I just started talking to Him there in the kitchen. I prayed something like:

"God, if You really exist, I need Your help. I am so close to making it big in the wrestling business. God, You know I am not connected like the second- and third-genera-

tion wrestlers. I have no political connections, If You help me become a superstar, I'll give back. The only way I am going to make it is with Your help. God, I am in this little house I can't afford, and I am putting my wife through hell. Please, God, help me. If You will help me, I will do good things for You. I will help little kids. I will even go to church like my brother Jeff. God, I'm desperate; I need Your help. Amen."

That was such a selfish prayer, but as I think back, it was an acknowledgement that God was there and that there were things that He could do that I couldn't do for myself. It was a beginning.

I am very grateful God hears the prayers of desperate people and helpless wrestlers. I think the prayer that was starting to be answered was coming from a small group of Christians in California who had decided to pray every day that Sue and I would come to faith in Christ. Hindsight usually gives most of us the perspectives of the workings

I thought maybe God and I could make a deal, so I just started talking to Him there in the kitchen. . . .

It was a beginning.

of God. At the time, I thought it was my deal-making with God that was opening the doors, but now I believe that all the prayers of those new Christians in my family at home were a major catalyst in heaven for our salvation.

Then from out of nowhere, the Hardee's fast food chain decided to use the wrestlers of the NWA to promote their restaurants opening all over the South. The chain put our pictures on plastic cups. Hardee's asked me to appear at the openings, and they paid me more than I was making in the ring to shake hands and sign autographs.

From this time forward, finances became less and less an issue for us. Rick Steiner and I wrestled as a tag team, and I began to work main event matches,

In the movie, we shot an exterior that had the old Hardee's design, but the interior of the Franklin, Tennessee, restaurant was being renovated. We needed another place to shoot Young Sting signing autographs at Hardee's. The good folks at the People's Church came to the rescue by allowing us to shoot in their pingpong room. Rob, the producer, and I played while the film crew shot the scene nearby. It was really fun to beat up the producer at pingpong— heh, heh, Rob!

being paired with the big names in the NWA, such as Ric Flair. Early on I realized that the culture of the NWA considered those of us who came from Cowboy Bill's world as second-class citizens, along with some of the other guys that came from several other territories that Mr. Crockett bought. This was Jim Crockett's big play to take on Vince McMahon and the then-WWF.

Mr. Crockett owned two airplanes—a very nice corporate jet and slower prop plane. I was still driving everywhere, and it occurred to me that I should get to ride on the plane because I was doing the main event matches. When I asked the road manager about it, he said "Sting, there is just no room on the planes; you will have to drive." So I drove three hundred miles to Hampton, Virginia, getting there just in time to get dressed for the main event. As I was getting ready to wrestle the champion "Nature Boy Ric Flair," another wrestler asked me why I wasn't on the plane. I told him that there were no seats, and he responded, "There was a seat open on the jet." That really frustrated me, and I told Ric Flair the story that night before we went on. I also told him what my contract was and found out I was making just ten percent of what many of the other NWA guys were making, even though they weren't doing the main events.

Ric said, "Don't worry, Sting. I'll take care of it." Later that night Mr. Crockett told me he would take care of my transportation problem and that I would notice a little something extra in my check.

I really started to have some fun when I got to the NWA. I had put in the time on the road to know what I was doing, and I got to start an ongoing feud for the NWA television championship. With Ric Flair's help I became part of the storyline for the Four Horsemen, one of the biggest attractions in all of wrestling. When I got kicked out of the Four Horsemen for disrespecting the Nature Boy Ric Flair, it set up a match with Ric for the World Championship. This feud with Ric Flair led to years of great storylines that were fun both for the fans and for us.

I started living at the La Quinta Hotel in Charlotte and spent almost a year and a half commuting between Dallas and Charlotte. I didn't want Sue to know what was happening in my life and kept telling her it wouldn't be much longer until the company moved its headquarters to Dallas. These years for Sue were really about waiting and hoping for us to be together, but as the relationship with TBS continued to grow it became less and less likely that the whole company would move to Texas.

In the 1990s the wrestling phenomenon took hold, and television audiences began to grow into the suburbs. Teenagers in the middle and upper-middle classes were beginning to embrace wrestling. College students were scheduling their weeks around wrestling. And the two biggest competitors in the market were the WWF—owned by Vince McMahon Jr., whose dad grew his wrestling empire along the East Coast—and the NWA, a distant second. I was wrestling every night, including Christmas and Thanksgiving. In the meantime, Sue got a job at a tack shop and was able to rekindle her long-standing love for horses. Eventually, she could afford her own horse.

Sue and I wanted children and wondered why we weren't getting pregnant, but the answer was very simple: I was never home. They say it is always darkest before the dawn, and my dark moment came when I was climbing back into the ring during a big cage match and something went wrong—my knee got blown out. If I'd been listening, I probably would have heard the voice of God saying softly, "Steve, I am going to slow you down so that you can hear Me and fall in love with your wife again." I, on the other hand, was worried about losing my place in the pecking order at the NWA and was totally focused on rehab. Sue was great during this time, and I did get back into wrestling shape in record time after the operation.

> In the 1990s the wrestling phenomenon took hold, and television audiences began to really grow into the suburbs.

Then came the break that every performer dreams of but seldom has the opportunity to achieve.

The Nature Boy Ric Flair was the champion and standard-bearer for the NWA. Ric is an amazing talent, and his reign as champion had a continual draw for the fans. Ric and I were scheduled to wrestle a championship bout on NWA's biggest TV show of the year, an event called The Great American Bash. He and I had worked together many times in main event matches around the country, and we had done a forty-five-minute match that had gotten an excellent television rating. Ric and I had chemistry in the ring that made our matches a real pleasure. The audience was on their feet the whole time, and the sound in the room was deafening. When my hand was raised as champion at the end of the match, the wrestling world—and my world—turned upside down. From that moment, the plane never left without me, and I finally could think about retiring the '83 T-Bird.

THE BIG RIDE

Jim Crockett was having a big time with his wrestling stable that included Lex Lugar, Ric Flair, Rick Steiner, the Four Horsemen, the Road Warriors, Midnight Express, the Rock and Roll Express, and now Sting. We were making a dent for two main reasons. First, we were developing personalities that the fans were really getting into, and this meant the crowds on the road were growing. Second, we had the power of Ted Turner's TBS, the Superstation.

Ted Turner came into broadcasting out of the original family business, billboards. They owned most of the great billboard space in the South and won the billboard wars by outflanking their competition over and over again. Now we were the number one show on Ted's air, but Jim Crockett owned us. If you have followed Mr. Turner's career at all, you know he is a very bold man. He built, paid for, and captained the sailboat that successfully defended the America's Cup. He bought the Braves baseball team, put them on his Superstation, and made people throughout the nation think of them as their team. He

also bought the Hawks basketball team. It
was a natural evolution for him to want to
own what was becoming the largest draw
on his network. He and Mr. Crockett made
a deal, and he bought all of the NWA.
They then changed the name to World
Championship Wrestling, and WCW was
born. Now there were only two real players
in the wrestling world—Vince McMahon's
WWF, which was the biggest player, and the new Turner-
sponsored WCW. And WCW's whole goal was to become
number one.

Immediately Vince started raiding our company by
painting a picture of the outrageous money there was to
be made for guys who would come over to WWF, but I
was too busy in those early days to worry much about the
war between Vince and Ted.

When the Turner deal finally came through I had no
reason not to move Sue to Atlanta, which was going to be
the capital city of the new WCW. I promised Sue a new
start in Atlanta with a bigger house and the real possibil-
ity of spending more time together. We were moving into

a neighborhood that included Lex Lugar and his wife, Peggy, who Sue really liked. So we loaded up the Blazer that had replaced the T-Bird and along with our cat, Mr. Bodine, we headed for Atlanta. That was a fun trip for us, and the hope of being together more really delighted Sue. The sad truth was that life in Dallas, even after we had more financial security, was one of the hardest times in our relationship. I would on occasion travel thirty-five days in a row without coming home. Sometimes the only way Sue and I would see each other would be if she came to the airport while I was passing through on my way to another match. Sue, in order to keep her own sanity, built a life that revolved

It was a natural evolution for Ted Turner to want to own what was becoming the largest draw on his network, so he bought the NWA and changed the name to World Championship Wrestling. WCW was born.

around riding and her equestrian friends. Sue even took in a female boarder who worked for the airlines because I was hardly ever home. This was a world of my making as I kept Sue distant from the wrestling life and realities that I wanted her never to know.

Sue's world revolved around horses; my world revolved around wrestling. The sad truth is that our worlds should have revolved around each other and the living God.

Then God did something that gave us meaning like we had never known as a couple. Sue got pregnant and our first son, Garrett, was born in 1990. Two years later our son Steven came along. Needless to say, Sue's life went through a drastic change, and having those little boys created a buffer to the lingering issues in our relationship. I truly loved the idea of being a dad even though in practical terms I wasn't. But even with our new sons who we loved so much, Sue and I really didn't get to the real issues that were driving us apart. The one passion we shared was loving our kids.

THE BREAKTHROUGH

Before Ted Turner, we were a wrestling company that produced television shows; after being acquired we were a television company that produced wrestling. It took years for that dust to settle. Wrestlers and CEOs at WCW came and went, but Ted Turner remained patient with us because he loved wrestling. I appreciated Mr. Turner's tenacious attitude.

Every Monday Vince McMahon had a primetime show called *Raw* that blazed a trail and changed all of wrestling. Ted's countermove was to bring in Eric Bischoff. Eric was hungry, loved wrestling, and had the right attitude for such fierce competition. He worked hard to understand the psychology of the audience. Some nights he would go into the crowd and listen to the people as the wrestlers were introduced, and in this way he would judge the popularity of each guy. Ted told Eric he wanted his own live show on TNT to rival *Raw*. This would give Ted wrestling shows on both his TBS and TNT networks. Vince's *Raw* was live one week and taped the next, so the fans would already know the outcome of the storyline before the pre-recorded show ever made air. We decided on the electricity and freshness that comes with being live every week. The fans had to tune in every time to know what would happen next. We called our event *Nitro*, and *Nitro* would define WCW. Before long *Nitro* was running neck and neck with *Raw*.

The other fun aspect of working for Eric was his openness to input and ideas. One of the best collaborative efforts between us happened as we were getting ready to launch *Nitro*.

The very first night that *Nitro* aired, we pulled off one of the biggest coups in wrestling history. Lex Lugar had been my tag-team partner in the NWA and the early WCW days before he defected to WWF with a lot of other wrestlers. He and I had remained friends and after a few years with the "other guys," he started saying to me privately that he might be ready to make a change. I thought that would be a great way to set the tone for the new *Nitro* show. And that is exactly what happened. We struck a secret deal for Lex to come to WCW; nobody knew except Eric and me. We kept Lex hidden until the last minute and when I introduced him to the crowd, the roof blew off the building. He had been due to be on Vince's *Raw* broadcast that same night, and they had no idea he had defected. Rumor has it Vince was looking for Lex backstage until his television people, who were monitoring our show, told him that Lex had just been introduced as a new member of WCW. I would have loved to be a fly on the wall that night to see Vince's reaction.

Wrestling was big business and changing very rapidly into not just a show, but a spectacle.

Eric welcomed input, and we wrestlers were able to contribute to the company creatively through ideas for storylines that seemed to get people really involved. One of the biggest ideas to ever come out of WCW was cooked up by Scott Hall and Kevin Nash. They called it the NWO (The New World Order). They changed their personas to the extreme and created a new, edgy look both in and out of the ring. They formed a

> *My original Sting character was the all-American West Coast surfer boy, but Sting as "the Crow" had become a vigilante out to right the wrongs that were happening in the world. This risk turned out to be the best move I'd ever made in my career.*

gang of wrestlers, who were more edgy than anyone had ever been. This was a group of renegades (in the storyline) who were against WCW.

Shortly after the NWO was born, I took a huge risk and decided to retire my original Sting persona, the blond flattop. My original Sting character had been the all-American hero, and Scott Hall suggested that I paint my whole face, not just part of it. We developed a storyline to launch my new look, and what emerged was a silent, mysterious persona. Sting as "the Crow" was now a vigilante out to right the wrongs that were happening. The last words I uttered in the ring for over a year were not long after I had premiered the Crow: "the only thing for sure about Sting is that nothing is for sure." The reinvention also allowed me to become an enforcer for both WCW and the NWO.

This risk paid huge dividends. Everyone was talking about Sting. Everybody wanted to know whether Sting was WCW or NWO. This risk turned out to be the best career move I had ever made. I started appearing in the rafters above the arenas, and people would look up and scream when they saw me. The next idea came from Eric who asked me to rappel out of the rafters and into the arena. We got a Hollywood stunt coordinator and he rigged me to fly. The debut came in Chicago with the ring below me about the length of a football field—297 feet. The ring looks really small from that height. I dropped into the arena and used a black baseball bat to bring justice to the situation What a great storyline that turned out to be! The rappel became part of my ongoing repetoire, and our television ratings and live show attendance skyrocketed. The question remained whether Sting was NWO or WCW. Then came a showdown where I was surrounded, and it was revealed that I had remained loyal to the WCW.

What everybody wanted to see was Sting verses Hogan, and in Starcade '97 we wrestled for the world championship.

Remember that guy named Terry, who came into my gym in California? Eric then persuaded wrestling's longest-reigning superstar, Hulk Hogan, to leave Vince in another huge coup for WCW. It gave our organization a boost and a lot of respect. With Hulk Hogan and the other great wrestling names who had chosen our company, we were the best wrestling show in the world.

Hulk was a guy who had gone places no wrestler had ever gone before and that no one has achieved since. But like all of us the Hulk had to reinvent himself; the wrestling fans were changing with the mood of the country, and they had began to tire of the "too good to be true" guy that was his persona. Hulk turned into Hollywood Hulk Hogan, and the NWO became his opportunity to turn to the dark side and make himself the guy you loved to hate. When he was added to the NWO they became the best bad men in the wrestling world—and the perfect targets for the dark superhero Sting. The NWO even built its own Sting character as part of their storyline. Their Sting was a bad guy who used my face paint, and this empha-sized how my character, the real Sting, was a lonely warrior fighting for right. I was the ultimate good guy, while Hulk was the ultimate bad guy.

Starcade '97 was the biggest pay per view event of all time. What started as a carnival sideshow had grown up to become a driving force in television.

The stage was being set for one of the biggest pay per view events in history. That whole buildup lasted about eighteen months, and the fans had a lot of fun wondering how it would turn out. Everybody wanted to see Sting take on Hollywood

Hulk Hogan, and an event called Starcade '97 was chosen for this titanic confrontation of hero and villain. When I walked through the curtain I knew nothing could get bigger or more intense than that moment in my wrestling life. We were soundly beating WWF in the ratings war every week, and this match captured fans' imagination like few other matches have, before or since. Everyone was watching, especially those WWF guys. What happened that night is wrestling and broadcast history. Hulk had a bad knee and my personal life was taking a major toll on me, but we realized this was momentous. Starcade '97 was, up to that time, the biggest pay per view event ever. That includes every sport and every other program up until then. Our match held that record

until it was finally broken by Wrestle Mania.

Then Scott Hall and Kevin Nash again broke ground as they reinvented the most successful storyline wrestling had ever seen. They formed the Wolfpac, which was the new version of the New World Order, and they tried to recruit me from my world of solitude into their new, red NWO gang. Being part of the Wolfpac, which included Scott Hall, Kevin Nash, Lex Lugar, the Macho Man Randy Savage, and Konan, created another ongoing storyline the fans fell in love with. After almost a year, I was persuaded to become Wolfpac, and the Sting persona changed to red war paint that resembled the black and white Sting. I was Wolfpac for a couple of years, and then a storyline came that got me back to black and white Sting, who is the character that everyone seems to identify with best.

Being able to assimilate and deliver all these storylines really captured the imagination of not only the fans, but also the wrestling press who began to refer to me as "the Franchise" for WCW, because I had stayed with the company and not given into the temptation to join WWF.

The former carnival sideshow had grown up into a driving force in mainstream television and in the pop culture as well. WCW/NWO wrestlers became the rock stars of the athletic world. But on the home front, Sue and I were drifting ever more distant as my double life on the road continued to grow darker and darker. Now I was completely out of control.

THE SUCCESS, THE FAILURE

Sting was everywhere. He was on the front of every major wrestling magazine, there was a Sting NASCAR, a Sting monster truck, and more then four hundred companies licensed the Sting image for everything from video games and action figures to air fresheners. Then there were major television appearances, a *TV Guide* cover, and a TNT movie of the week. The WCW family of talent began to really work as the wrestlers built their own identities. Every week we would line up head to head our *Nitro* against *Raw*, and we were taking the ratings battle to WWF.

Here is what happened every night after a big WCW event: All the wrestlers would step into the hotel lobby where we were staying, and a crowd of fans would be wanting autographs, or just wanting to glimpse their favorite ring gladiators. Also, part of the bar or restaurant would be blocked off for us. Most wrestlers are over-the-top people in the ring, and as a rule this translates into a very hard-living, egocentric lifestyle. Night after night, week after week, year after year, the party rolled on.

Night after
night, week
after week, year
after year, the
party rolled on.

During this time I had a very tough time sleeping; there were years of nights when I hardly slept at all. Recently someone asked whether the pain of taking bumps in the ring is what really made me get into drinking and taking prescription drugs, but the truth is that I was in a place that is often described as "the dark night of the soul." I was dealing with such guilt, wanting to do right thing but not having the strength to do it on my own. This reminded me of the relaxation and sleep-escape I had while taking prescription pain killers and muscle relaxers during my recuperation from a blown-out knee. As I continued to run from God, my dark life of rebellion turned to a mixture of prescription drugs and alcohol, a combo that would anesthetize my conscience and let me escape into sleep. This turned from occasional, to frequent, to a must have, in order for me to sleep at all.

RUNNING FROM MEANING

With my "so-called" superstar lifestyle in full rush, people
back in California were still praying for me every day.

The status did not fill the void in my soul, the fame
did not fill the void in my soul, and the stuff did not fill
the void in my soul. I was running, but I was running on
empty and really didn't know why. People kept trying to
tell me about God. I believed at that time it was all coin-
cidence, but I began to realize the truth of God's pursuit
of my soul.

I was running,
but I was running on empty
and really didn't know why.

THE TURN

My brother Jeff had continued to grow in the Lord, and I watched his life intently. When he first got saved, his all-or-nothing approach to his faith made our relationship awkward, and from time to time he just ticked me off. But the more I viewed his consistency over the years of walking with the Lord, I began to realize he had something that I just didn't have. I was drawn to Jeff in a way that went beyond our relationship as brothers. I really had not spent much time recognizing the supernatural power of God in any aspect of my life, but it was there quietly tugging at me, turning me to face my Creator in a way I never had before.

Then other wrestlers began to talk to me about the truth they knew about God.

One guy told me a what-if story while we were hanging out together one day. He'd heard it from his pastor one Sunday at church. He said: "Imagine you are flying on a jumbo jet that suddenly starts plummeting to earth. What would you do?" Most people in the congregation had said they would ask God for forgiveness for their sins and make sure they were ready for eternity. Then the pastor had asked everyone to imagine that the pilot was able to get control of the plane and land safely. "Would you remember what you promised God? Would your life change, or would you just fall back into your old ways and forget what you'd promised God." At that point I started to squirm and told the wrestler I'd heard enough.

Former WWF champion Ted "Million Dollar Man" Dibiase became my friend after I got my hands on his book, *Every Man Has His Price,* and devoured it. In the book Ted recounts his journey from wrestling's bad boy to his new life in Christ. I identified with his story, and this was another seed God planted.

I am so grateful that God was going to do whatever it took to break me so He could remake me.

> *I had not spent much time recognizing*
> *the supernatural power of God in any aspect*
> *of my life, but it was there quietly tugging at me,*
> *turning me to face my Creator.*

Then one time I was walking through a hotel lobby after a big WCW event when this really big guy and a couple of his buddies stopped me as I was on my way to the airport. He introduced himself to me as Simeon Nix, a friend of Ted D's and the worship leader at Bell Shoals Baptist Church. Simeon said he heard that I had been going to church a little bit. Then he asked, "Sting, would you mind if my friends and I pray with you?" There we were in the hotel lobby with people everywhere, and I was sweating bullets. My attention was not on this good brother's prayer but on the elevator doors. I thought, "What if Ric Flair or the Four Horsemen or some of my other guys come through here right now? What will they think?" Then I thought, "The next time I see Ted, I am going to hit him right in the mouth." When Simeon finished his prayer, I quickly excused myself and headed for the door, but as I was scurrying away Simeon called, "Hey, Sting, if that plane goes down, do you know where you will spend eternity?"

This time I couldn't shake the wondering: "*What if*

> *I am so grateful that God was going to do whatever it took to break me so He could remake me.*

the plane goes down? Is that all there is, or is the message of Christ real? What is God trying to tell me?"

On a trip home to California, Sue and I went with Jeff and his family to church, where Jeff was an elder. The pastor invited people to receive Christ at the conclusion of the service. I got all emotional, and both Sue and I raised our hands in acceptance. Then we walked out of church and nothing changed.

When we returned to Atlanta I began to think that maybe I needed some different influences if I was going to really get my life together. Jeff and his family seemed to be doing it right, and it was obvious they had something we didn't have. I felt that if we could just be near my family, who knew the Lord, then maybe some of that would rub off on Sue and me. I was so out of control and desperate for change. I told Sue we should move back to California. Sue had wanted to go back to California, but for years I had told her we would never go back because I couldn't see us raising our family there. My about-face was hard for her, but once again I promised that I would be a better husband because of the influence of my brother and the rest of the family. For Sue, this

I was out of control and desperate for change.

was the last-ditch effort to salvage whatever we had left. So once again we loaded up the moving van.

Soon after we moved back to California, we noticed how happy and obedient Jeff and Lori's kids were, so Sue and I asked Jeff their secret to raising such great kids. He told us that he and Lori taught a parenting class called Growing Kids God's Way, and they offered to teach us these classes once a week in their home. It was revolutionary for Sue and me as a guideline in raising our children, and we noticed immediate results. We were like a lot of people who might see the right thing to do for their children, but then don't apply the lessons to their own lives.

About a year later, Jeff asked if I would go with him, Dad, and Mark to a Promise Keepers event in Los Angeles. I had never seen so many men who were singing together and listening to other men talk about faith and priorities and families. It really got under my skin. I had not been paying attention to my relationship with Sue, and the skeletons were really rattling in my closet. The guilt was unbearable. When the time for the invitation came I was standing next to my brother Mark, who is a Christian now but at the time was a little sarcastic, and he made fun of the invitation to receive Christ.

I went down front again anyway. Something in me had not clicked the first time, and I still felt I was not there as far as the Lord was concerned. I kept thinking, "Maybe this time it will stick." Everyone in the family was freaking out that I had gone down front and prayed to receive Christ.

But the superstar lifestyle continued as usual. The next Monday I was back in Atlanta on *Nitro* with 20 million people watching.

THE MOMENT OF TRUTH

The next twelve months were some of the biggest in my career, and at the same time God continued to work on me through Jeff, Ted Dibiase, and others.

The truth is that I was trying to deal with God instead of surrendering to Him. The Bible tells how "godly sorrow produces repentance" (2 Corinthians 7:10). I felt sick about my sin, but it is not enough to know that sin is wrong; what God wants to teach us is how to hate sin the way He does. Our sin sent His Son to be executed in our place. I would die for my children. I can't imagine the pain of a parent who loses a child—but somehow in God's plan that is what He endured for me. God gave up His only Son to pay for the sin that I had committed. As that truth sunk in, I realized I needed to not only want to go to heaven and miss hell, but I needed to feel the sorrow that comes through the realization of what my sin did to Jesus.

Many of us sat in horror-filled silence as we watched *The Passion of the Christ* unfold before our eyes in the

magnificent film produced by our brother Mel Gibson. The suffering depicted on the screen is only a fraction of the real story as "He who knew no sin [became] sin for us, that we might become the righteousness of God in Him" (2 Corinthians 5:19).

Soon after we arrived in California we went on a rare family vacation to Hawaii. For the first time in our married life Sue looked through my luggage, and she found a large bottle of prescription drugs. Sue had asked me in the past if I was using drugs, and I had denied it. This time I told her I had trouble sleeping, and she bought me herbal tea and other natural methods to help me with my insomnia; she was totally unaware of my dependence on the deadly combination of prescription drugs and alcohol for getting any sleep at all. The thought of going for a week without any artificial help motivated me to bring the bottle on our trip. She was shocked and hurt when she found them, but now I am glad she did. This happened the first day we got to the Islands, and for the rest of the trip we barely spoke. We tried to have a good time with the kids, but my stupidity built a cold distance between us. I made Sue give me back the bottle, and by the time we got home it was empty.

Shortly after we returned from Hawaii, Sue and I

were alone in the house while the boys were playing with friends. We had hardly spoken since the trip. Sue confronted me and said, "You lied to me about the prescription drugs.

Is there anything else I need to know that you have kept a secret from me?" This was the moment that was ordained by God Himself.

I was trying to deal with God instead of surrendering to Him.

For everyone the Moment of Truth takes a different shape. For me it was facing up to my betrayal of my wife and family for all those years while I was trying to make it big, and then when I did, how my sin just kept right on. There was no gratefulness in my heart; there was nothing but what Steve wanted, not what God wanted. I couldn't stop the word from coming and I answered, "Yes." That opened the floodgate of repentance that God had been waiting for—true sorrow for my sin, and a true belief that Jesus would cleanse me from "all unrighteousness." The truth truly does set you free. Suddenly the weight was of the world was off my shoulders. I confessed to Sue my dark past, and the realization that my sins were forgiven filled me with hope. But I might as well have driven a dagger into my wife's heart. Sue got answers to questions that she had been afraid to

For godly sorrow produces repentance
leading to salvation, not to be regretted;
but the sorrow of the world produces death.
For observe this very thing,
that you sorrowed in a godly manner:
What diligence it produced in you,
what clearing of yourselves,
what indignation, what fear,
what vehement desire, what zeal,
what vindication!
In all things you proved yourselves
to be clear in this matter.

1 CORINTHIANS 7:10, 11

If we confess our sins,
He is faithful and just to forgive us our sins
and to cleanse us from all unrighteousness.

1 John 1:9

ask, and I begged her to forgive me.

Many times during this process the devil kept accusing me of the sins for which I had been forgiven. This is one of the devil's big tactics in trying to discourage new Christians. He wants us to believe that what we did was just too bad and that God could never ever forgive us. But the people who God had put in my life reminded me that God is trustworthy and that when He says your sins are cleansed, He means it. They're gone.

For Sue, the revelations of that day were her worst fears about our relationship and the double life I had lived for so long. But God put a fresh love for Sue in my heart, and I was willing to do anything to be a husband and father who would honor God and win back the family I had treated with such disregard.

This began a renewal in our relationship that did not happen overnight. As you can imagine, Sue was very hurt and angry and justifiably so. I don't know what I expected,

Sue's question opened the floodgate of repentance that God was waiting for—true sorrow for my sin, and a true belief that Jesus would cleanse me of all unrighteousness. This was a horrible, wonderful day.

> *God put a fresh love for Sue in my heart, and I was willing to do anything to be a husband and father who would honor God and win back the family I had treated with such disregard.*

maybe that God would wave a magic wand and everything would be perfect. But instead my confession created a whirlwind in my home that could only be repaired through the miracle of God's grace. Sue wanted me to leave and never wanted to see me again. I begged her to let me stay. I had to leave that first night, and Sue then agreed to let me back in the house because of the kids. From that act of grace on her part, we began to rebuild our broken relationship brick by brick, and God began to work His healing in our relationship. That painful day, with all its regret on my part, was the step that started Sue on her own journey to forgiveness and the full establishment of our marriage on the absolute truth of God and full disclosure.

Now, not only did I have to face my wife and deal with my sin, but I also felt the definite prompting of God to tell the guys at WCW what had happened to me and that I had become a fully devoted follower of Christ. These same guys had known me for many years, and they clearly understood the

dark side of my life. Now I had to tell them what Jesus had done in my life and that I was a changed man.

I went to the guys individually and in small groups, including Hulk Hogan, Ric Flair, Scott and Rick Steiner, and my boss, Eric Bishoff. Most of them said they understood and wished me well, but others just didn't get it at all. They thought I had become a religious nut case.

In 2000, the year Gracie Borden was born as a ray of sunshine to our whole family, rumors started to fly that Ted Turner was going to spin off WCW. Eric Bishoff put together a group to buy the company, and I was very excited about being involved in that new concern. At the last minute our old rival, Vince McMahon, swooped in and bought WCW. March 27, 2001 was the final *Nitro*, and it seemed fitting that the last match in WCW history was the Nature Boy Ric Flair against Sting.

I had come to Christ, and now I had the choice of wrestling in WWF (now WWE) or investing in the family I had put in second place so often.

God's plan is always perfect, and He knew what I

> When God says your sins are cleansed, He means it. They're gone.

needed most was time with Sue and my family. He also knew I needed to develop a whole new circle of relationships with people who believe the Bible is the Word of God and who live by its standards. He had given me a real desire to know His Word and to share my faith. My family surrounded me with love and godly concern that helped Sue and me weather the

It seemed fitting that the last match in WCW history was the Nature Boy Ric Flair against Sting.

storm. We still have a long way to go, but Sue and I are committed to serving God with all our hearts. The past occasionally still pains our relationship, but God is slowly erasing the memories of those days and is replacing them with the joy that comes with knowing we are walking with Him.

In the world of wrestling, there is always a storyline that involves the audience in the match. Similarly, in this life all of us are playing out our individual storylines before the Living God who calls us from our lives of sin. He is the Creator of the universe, and He calls us into relationship with His only Son, Jesus Christ, who paid the price for sin with His own life in exchange for ours. My hope for you is that you if you don't know Jesus, then you will open your heart to Him right now.

Jesus came to earth to express the love of God directly to you by shedding His blood on a Roman cross and dying so that you would not have to pay the price a holy God demanded for your sin— "for the wages of is death . . ." (Romans 6:23). God expressed His love to the whole world through sending Jesus to die for all the sin that has ever existed and He showed His awesome saving power over death and sin through the resurrection of Jesus from the dead. ". . . but the gift of God is eternal life through Jesus Christ our Lord" (Romans 6:23).

The God of the universe wants to communicate with you personally. If you refuse to repent and ask God to forgive you of your sin, then you will receive the wages for your sin which is death. "But God demonstrates His own love toward us, in that while we were still sinners, Christ died for us" (Romans 5:8). "God loved the world so much that He gave His one and only Son so that whoever believes in him may not be lost, but have eternal life" (John 3:16 NCV).

My hope for you
is that if you don't know Jesus,
you will open your heart
to him right now.

It took me fifteen years to understand what I have just

explained to you.

So what are you going to do about it? What will be

the end of your storyline? Will you live, die, and pay the

price for sin, which is death and hell. Or will you confess

your sin and accept the forgiveness that Jesus has already

paid for on the cross?

I pray you will make your decision for Christ right

now and experience your own **Moment of Truth**.

A Note from Steve Borden

With special thanks:

To George and Kathy King,
for believing in me, your patience and professionalism.
I am blessed to know you.

To Jack and Marsha Countryman and the staff
at J. Countryman books, for this opportunity
and your enthusiasm about the book.

To Rob Venneri, your friendship means so much.
Thank you for your support and sense of humor.

To my family, for your unconditional love and prayers.

To my brother Jeff, for helping me
rebuild the bridge, one brick at a time.

To my wife Sue, thank you for your trust, your love,
and your patience. There are no words to describe
my love for you. You are the love of my life. I.N.G.U!

To God, for restoring my marriage,
my family and my life.

. . . sb

A Note from George King

I wish to thank Jack and Marsha Countryman, with whom my wife, Kathryn, and I teach Sunday school at the People's Church of Franklin Tennessee. Jack and Marsha have followed the production of the film *Sting: Moment of Truth* from its inception. As the first edits of the movie started to emerge we began to kick around the idea of a book that would chronicle the making of the movie, but even more would tell this amazing story of God's grace. I called Steve Borden a.k.a. Sting and shared with him Jack's belief that his story needed to be told, and Steve agreed that we should go for it. That was in July 2004, and the book needed to be on the street by November 1—an impossible task. Thus began a writing 100-yard dash that is the book you hold in your hands. Fortunately, I had written the screenplay for the movie, so the story was fresh for me. Then came many all-nighters on the phone with Steve and Sue Borden as they became comfortable with what we wanted the book to be. Our editor Kathy Baker has been a great encourager and gently pushed the book along to make it a reality. My hat is off to the whole J. Countryman team who tackled a project we all believed in and got the job done. I am grateful to my old friend Jerry Park and the Thomas Nelson sales organization, for they are the unsung heroes of the story as they made sure this book got everywhere.

I also should thank some people who have put up with me during the rush to the finish line. First my wife, Kathryn, who encouraged me endlessly, even to the point of letting me write the book during the first vacation we'd had in two years. My partners, Robert Venneri and Rick Wackeen, who allowed me to do double-duty as movie director/producer and book writer. And I especially would like to thank my friends Steve and Sue Borden, who worked tirelessly with me to make the story of their journey to faith in Christ so transparent and inspiring. Their courage will result in many lives being transformed by the power of the living God. I am an honored participant in this book that I know was ordained to make a difference. Until He comes . . . gk

A MOVIE OF POWER, PAIN & ULTIMATE TRIUMPH

STING

MOMENT OF TRUTH

DVD

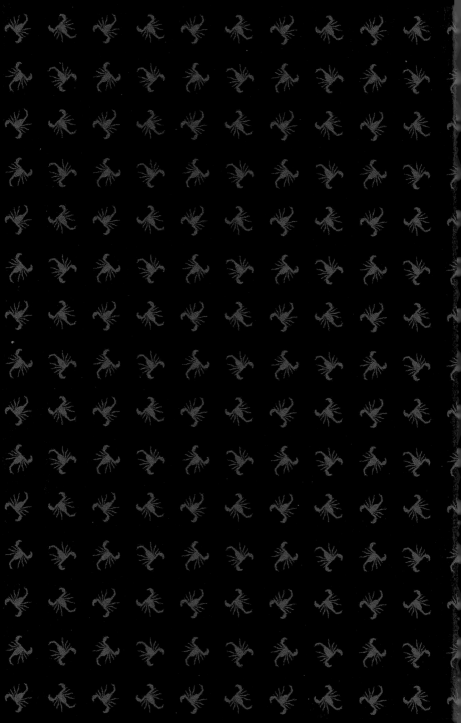